Pebble® Plus

Look Inside Animal Homes

Look Inside a Robin's Nest

by Megan Cooley Peterson

Consulting Editor: Gail Saunders-Smith, PhD

Consultant: Anne R. Hobbs
Public Information Specialist
Cornell Lab of Ornithology
Ithaca, New York

CAPSTONE PRESS
a capstone imprint

Pebble Plus is published by Capstone Press,
151 Good Counsel Drive, P.O. Box 669, Mankato, Minnesota 56002.
www.capstonepub.com

Books published by Capstone Press are manufactured with paper
containing at least 10 percent post-consumer waste.

Library of Congress Cataloging-in-Publication Data
Peterson, Megan Cooley.
  Look inside a robin's nest / by Megan Cooley Peterson.
    p. cm.—(Pebble plus. Look inside animal homes)
  Includes bibliographical references and index.
  Summary: "Full-color photographs and simple text describe robin nests"—Provided by publisher.
  ISBN 978-1-4296-6077-8 (library binding)
  1. Robins—Habitations—Juvenile literature. 2. Nest building—Juvenile literature. I. Title.
QL696.P2P48 2012
598.8'42—dc22   2011000265

Editorial Credits
Katy Kudela, editor; Gene Bentdahl, designer; Marcie Spence, media researcher; Laura Manthe, production specialist

Photo Credits
Alamy Images: Frank Paul, cover, Mark Romesser 11 (inset), Stone Nature Photography, 13; iStockphoto:
CherylEDavis, 5, JamesBrey, 19, Michael Reynolds, 11, pazzophoto, 1; Minden Pictures: S. D. K. Maslowski, 17;
Photo Researchers, Inc.: Kenneth H. Thomas, 7; Shutterstock: DD Photography, 15, Kevin E. Beasley, 9,
Pavel Cheiko, 21

Note to Parents and Teachers

The Look Inside Animal Homes series supports national science standards related to life
science. This book describes and illustrates robins' nests. The images support early readers
in understanding the text. The repetition of words and phrases helps early readers learn new
words. This book also introduces early readers to subject-specific vocabulary words, which are
defined in the Glossary section. Early readers may need assistance to read some words and to
use the Table of Contents, Glossary, Read More, Internet Sites, and Index sections of the book.

Printed in the United States of America in North Mankato, Minnesota.
032011   006110CGF11

Table of Contents

A Home for Young Robins

A robin's nest is a home

for young robins.

Between three and four

chicks live in one nest.

Building a Robin's Nest

Each spring female robins

build nests in forests and towns.

They build nests on

tree branches, in shrubs,

and other places.

Female robins build their nests

in three to 10 days.

They gather twigs,

roots, and grass.

Female robins shape the twigs,

roots, and grass into cups.

They add mud to the

inside of the nests.

Mud makes the nests strong.

Female robins place

soft grass over the mud.

A finished nest is 3 inches

(7.6 centimeters) tall.

It is 6 inches (15 cm) wide.

Inside a Robin's Nest

Robin nests are open on top.

Robins hop into their nests.

Females lay blue eggs inside.

Female robins sit

on their eggs

for two weeks.

They keep the eggs safe

and warm until they hatch.

Chicks live in the nests

for only two weeks.

But parents care for them

after they leave the nests.

Females may lay more eggs.

In winter all robins

gather together to

live in roosts.

Female robins will build

new nests in spring.

Glossary

chick—a very young bird

hatch—to break out of an egg

roost—a place where birds gather at night to rest; robin roosts can be found in forests and swamps

root—the part of a plant or tree that grows under the ground

shrub—a plant or bush with woody stems that branch out near the ground

twig—a small, thin branch of a tree or other woody plant

Read More

Adamson, Heather. *Bird Nests*. Our Animal World. Mankato, Minn.: Amicus, 2011.

Nelson, Robin. *Robins*. Animal Life Cycles. Minneapolis: Lerner Publications, 2009.

Internet Sites

FactHound offers a safe, fun way to find Internet sites related to this book. All of the sites on FactHound have been researched by our staff.

Here's all you do:

Visit *www.facthound.com*

Type in this code: 9781429660778

Super-cool stuff! Check out projects, games and lots more at
www.capstonekids.com

Index

Word Count: 180
Grade: 1
Early-Intervention Level: 13